How Birds Eat

Trace Taylor

Robbie Byerly

This is a bird.

ostrich

bee-eater

white-faced ducks

All of these are birds.

Birds eat many things. Birds eat in many ways.

Some birds eat what other birds can't.

These are seeds. Some birds eat seeds.

nut

seed

Seeds can be in nuts.

This is a parrot. Parrots like to eat seeds like these.

These seeds are in big hard nuts.

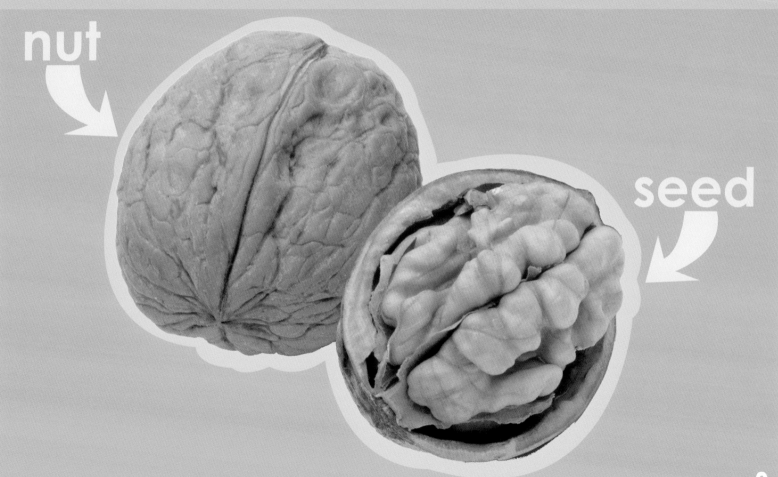

nut

seed

The parrot has to break the nut to get the seed.

This is the parrot's beak. Its beak is big.
It is made to break big nuts.

Look at the parrot's tongue.

Its tongue helps it pull the seed out of the nut.

This is how parrots can eat big seeds many other birds can't.

Some birds eat bugs.

This bird eats bees.
It is a bee-eater.

stinger

Bees can sting. Bees sting with their stingers.
The bee-eater does not want the bee to sting it.

The bee-eater catches the bee in its beak.

It slams the bee on a rock.

The stinger breaks off.

Now the bee-eater can eat the bee.

Some birds eat animals.

This is a hawk. Hawks eat these animals.

These are the hawk's claws.

Hawks use their sharp claws
to catch animals to eat.

This is the hawk's beak. It is very sharp, too.

The hawk's beak helps it tear away meat to eat.

Hawks have sharp claws and beaks. They can catch and eat animals that other birds can't.

All birds have to eat. All birds eat to live.
They use what they have to eat what they can.

BIRD FACTS and ADAPTATIONS

The environment in which an animal species lives influences its physical shape. For birds, the shape and size of their beaks, claws, tongues, heads, and bodies have often evolved specifically because they give a species advantages in acquiring its particular food.

Name: Macaw *(a kind of parrot)*
Habitat: Tropical regions of North and South America
Diet: Seeds, nuts, fruits, flowers, and leaves
Eating Habits
Macaws use their beaks to crack open nuts and seeds as well as to help them move around trees in search of other food.

Name: Bee-eater
Habitat: Tropical and subtropical Eurasia and Africa
Diet: Bees, wasps, dragonflies, moths, and other insects
Eating Habits
The bee-eater's long, hard beak protects it from the sting of the insects that it eats. Its beak also makes it easier to break off the stingers so the insects can be safely swallowed.

Name: Hawk
Habitat: All continents excluding Antarctica
Diet: Birds, small mammals, reptiles, and insects
Eating Habits
The hawk follows its prey as the prey tries to get away. It then grabs the prey with its strong talons. The hawk uses its sharp beak to rip apart the prey once it has killed it. The hawk is very important in controlling small-rodent populations.

Name: Gull
Habitat: More than 30 species in the Northern Hemisphere
Diet: Insects, crabs, worms, fish, eggs, and garbage
Eating Habits
Gulls will eat according to where they are and the activity around them. They will eat worms and bugs when near farms, and fish and crustaceans when near the water.

Name: Tanager
Habitat: Tropical forests in North and South America
Diet: Mostly fruit and some insects
Eating Habits
Tanagers have a small toothed and hooked beak. They eat mostly fruits, and some species are known to eat insects.

Name: Kingfisher
Habitat: Found worldwide—mainly in tropical climates
Diet: Fish, crustaceans, and lizards
Eating Habits
The kingfisher sits on its favorite perch and watches the water below. When it sees a fish it dives down very quickly, goes under the water, and stabs the fish. The kingfisher then brings the fish back to its perch and beats it against the rocks before eating it.

Name: Hummingbird
Habitat: North and South America
Diet: Nectar and insects
Eating Habits
Hummingbirds have a long, slim bill. This allows them to reach deep into certain flowers to get the nectar. The bill can be up to half the overall length of the entire bird.

Use the words you know
to read new words...

am	eat	day	see
ham	meat	may	fee
slam	beat	say	feed
slams	beak	way	seed

Tricky Words

other   pull   help   catch   away